Patios, Porches, & Verandas

ROCKPORT

Patios, Porches, & Verandas

GLOUCESTER MASSACHUSETTS

ROCKPORT PUBLISHERS

Copyright © 2006 by LOFT Publications

First published in the United States of America by
Rockport Publishers, a member of
Quayside Publishing Group
33 Commercial Street
Gloucester, MA 01930-0589
Telephone: (978) 282-9590
Fax: (978) 283-2742
www.rockpub.com

ISBN: 1-59253-281-0

Editor:
Ana Cañizares

Art Director:
Mireia Casanovas Soley

Graphic Design and Layout:
Oriol Serra Juncosa

Editorial project:
2006 © **LOFT Publications**
Via Laietana 32, 4th Of. 92.
08003 Barcelona. Spain
Tel.: +34 932 688 088
Fax: +34 932 687 073
loft@loftpublications.com
www.loftpublications.com

Printed in Spain

Contents

Patios

Porches

Verandas

O Exterior residential spaces have evolved throughout history and more recently become a key architectural component of residential design. Among the variety of typologies that exist today, many are inspired by traditional structures and often reinterpreted to create charming and contemporary outdoor spaces. This book devotes special attention to patios, porches, and verandas to display the endless possibilities offered by these kinds of spaces through the imaginative use of materials, textures, furnishings, and decorative accessories. Typical to warmer climates and rural areas, porches, patios, and verandas are especially present in colonial architecture and were originally inspired by traditional ethnic dwellings. In places like the south of the United States, for example, the veranda is considered as an emblematic feature of the local architecture and a frequently used area of the home. These outdoor spaces are often referred to as intermediate, given that they

are neither interior nor fully exterior; situated within an architectural frame-work, they are carefully planned and incorporate structural elements, a defined layout, and a series of accessories that can include anything from plants to furnishings. Designed to function as additional living spaces, they should provide the qualities necessary to fulfill this purpose, such as adequate lighting and ventilation, comfortable furnishings, attractive views, and a logical relationship with the interior. In this way, exterior areas must create the sense of security and comfort associated with being indoors. The use of structural elements and accessories that are commonly found inside a home can create this feeling of enclosure and containment. The following pages are filled with images of patios, porches, and verandas around the world that illustrate the many ways you can enhance your own outdoor space and integrate it within your home.

Patios

○ Borrowed from Spanish, the word patio originally described a roofless inner court typically found in Spanish or Spanish-American houses. Outside Spain, this term translates as a courtyard and can also refer to a paved area adjoining a house. This outdoor space, which can also adopt the appearance of a garden through the integration of plants and grass, is generally used for dining or recreation and usually situated in the center or rear of the house plan. Patios are typically made of concrete or stone slabs laid over a firm base composed of a layer of compacted hardcore (stone chips), a layer of sharp sand, and a layer of cement mortar. The firmness and stability of the base is essential to the robustness of the top layer of slabs; a weak base will typically result in a cracked surface. Therefore, patios that hold a lot of weight, such as driveways, require stronger foundations than those designed for light use. Other pavement surfaces include stone, pebbles, concrete, tile, terrazzo, or wood. Given the open character of this kind of space, particular consideration should be taken with regards to its orientation and the type of plants and furnishings that are chosen. The absence of a roof structure, in the case of extremely warm climates, may necessitate the integration of mobile sunshades or umbrellas, and a careful choice of plants that adapt to the given conditions. This chapter unfolds with a selection of patios that range from small inner courtyards to open, landscaped gardens that function as recreational areas.

This outdoor dining table integrates a large umbrella to provide diffused light and adequate shade on warm days.

© Eduardo Consuegra

© Eduardo Consuegra

Located in Colombia and designed by Guillermo Arias and Luis Cuartas, this house features a large interior patio with diverse areas defined by the use of different materials, such as wood, stone pebbles, and concrete.

© Reto Guntli/Zapaimages

© Reto Guntli/Zapaimages

© James Mitchell/Redcover.com

© Reto Guntli/Zapaimages

© Adam Butler

© Adam Butler

A large structural wall protects this patio space from the most intense hours of sunlight and also creates a more intimate environment.

© Cesar Rubio

© Cesar Rubio

Composed of large concrete slabs, this patio, situated adjacent to a bedroom, is complemented by a small pond with large rocks at the far end of the rectangular space.

© Ken Hayden/Redcover.com

A wide variety of materials and structures can be used to enclose a patio, such as these wooden screens that provide privacy without obstructing light and views.

© Hans Pattist

© Hans Pattist

This patio designed, by NIO Architecten, consists of an interior courtyard that captures natural daylight and distributes it around the residence.

© Hans Pattist

Full-height sliding glass doors permit a maximum entry of light, while a translucent glass screen ensures privacy from neighboring terraces.

© Hans Pattist

© Jordi Miralles

This small and simple patio serves as a
transitional space from the interior of the
home to the exterior garden.

© Gogortza/Llorella

© Sunset Magazine

This sustainably built prefabricated house
is called the Sunset Breezehouse due to its
outdoor-oriented configuration and
naturally cross-ventilated courtyards.

© Shinji Kogo

Architectural studio Atelier.Rats created
this contemporary outdoor space which,
thanks to its configuration, generates a
more intimate atmosphere.

© Bruno Klomfar

© Bruno Klomfar

42

© Matteo Piazza

This slightly elevated platform was situated at the border of an inclined terrain and adorned with cushions and mats to ensure a comfortable and soothing viewing experience.

The simplicity of this patio is aimed at embracing the stunning landscape and making the most of its privileged location.

© Winfried Heinze/Redcover.com

This residence was configured so that
various spaces have access to the central
patio, including the living area, corridor,
and main bedroom.

© Winfried Heinze/Redcover.com

© Henry Wilson/Redcover.com

© Henry Wilson/Redcover.com

Surrounding a patio with abundant
vegetation can be a practical and attractive
solution to unpleasant views or adjoining
neighbors.

© James Silverman/Redcover.com

Rooftop terraces are also considered a patio given their lack of an integrated ceiling. This patio deck incorporates a circular window that functions as an interior skylight.

© Simon McBride/Redcover.com

Introducing large planters can give patios,
especially those located within the city, a
more organic feel.

© James Mitchell/Redcover.com

Small stone pebbles offer an alternative to concrete, wood, and tile as a floor surface. Decorative details and soft textures can create a homely effect such as this one.

A large glass window allows the exterior
patio to become an attractive visual
element from within the home.

© Ken Hayden/Redcover.com

Pivoting panels can provide an interesting
alternative to sliding glass doors as a
separating element from interior to exterior.

© Ken Hayden/Redcover.com

© Henry Wilson/Redcover.com

The abundant sunlight received by this
patio allowed for the addition of numerous
plants, which were placed along the borders
and around a small table with benches.

© Ken Hayden/Redcover.com

Patios such as this one—designed to be used as living spaces—must make use of resistant materials and appropriate plants.

© Ken Hayden/Redcover.com

This patio features a waterfall integrated
into a brick wall that spills into a small
pond bordered by diverse plants.

Porches

O A porch is a classic architectural feature that consists of a floor-like platform structure attached to the front or back entrance of a residence. The paved area commonly integrates a roof structure designed to provide shade and protection from the sun or rain. In effect, this forms an extra exterior room that may accommodate chairs, tables, and other furniture, in order to be used as a living space. Situated along the external walls of the main building, a porch can also be enclosed by a screen, latticework, broad windows, or other walls extending from the main structure. This space can function simply as a transitional area in which to pause comfortably before entering or exiting the home, or as a complementary living area that benefits from pleasant climatic conditions. The porch, especially in the southern United States, is often as broad as it is deep, and may provide sufficient space for residents to entertain guests or gather on special occasions. The term is often interchanged with veranda, although the porch usually has a more open character. The porches shown here vary from rustic to contemporary, demostrating how the use of different materials such as wood, cement, or steel can generate very different effects in terms of style and form.

Wicker furnishings are a popular choice for outdoor spaces given their durability and easy maintenance.

© Adreas von Einsiedel

© Ricardo Labougle

The dominant use of wood generates a warm
atmosphere and integrates the architectural
structure with the surrounding landscape.

© Mark York/Redcover.com

© Ken Hayden/Redcover.com

81

© Miquel Tres

A porch can also take the form of an
independent structure to take advantage of
a large open space either at the front or at
the rear of a home.

© Miquel Tres

© Miquel Tres

© Miquel Tres

© Miquel Tres

© Miquel Tres

87

© Jordi Sarrà

The exterior area of the house that receives the most shade was chosen to create an outdoor living area in which to cool off during hot summer days.

© Reto Guntli/Zapaimages

© Reto Guntli/Zapaimages

Warm climates allow for year-round
outdoor spaces such as this one in Bali,
which functions as an interior living space
despite the absence of doors and the
openings in the roof.

© Reto Guntli/Zapaimages

© Reto Gundi/Zapaimages

97
Porches

© Gogortza/Llorella

This garden and porch, designed by
dos A dos Arquitectura del Paisatge and
RB Arquitectes, incorporates a paved area
composed of an arrangement of tiles. The
ceiling offers protection and shade to the
living and dining area.

© Gogortza/Llorella

© Andrea Martiradonna

© Craig Fraser/Redcover.com

Decorative structural details and the use of
materials such as tile and wicker produce a
distinguished feeling that is reminiscent of
traditional homes.

© Ken Hayden/Redcover.com

The combination of styles adds contrast and character. This country home built in stone features a contemporary wood dining table and a ceiling made of reed.

© Simon McBride/Redcover.com

The presence of climbing plants and wild
vegetation can provide further privacy and
shade to exterior living and dining areas.
The rural setting of this house is integrated
into the outdoor spaces through the
dominating presence of trees, shrubs, and
potted plants.

© Simon McBride/Redcover.com

© Simon McBride/Redcover.com

© Simon McBride/Redcover.com

© Simon McBride/Redcover.com

The upper terrace of this grand residence, supported by two pairs of columns, extends out over the lower terrace, situated slightly above ground level.

© Sargent Architectural Photography

This residence in Palm Beach incorporates a
classical porch featuring a roof structure
supported by columns.

© Colin Sharp/Redcover.com

This porch uses wooden blinds to create a more private and enclosed space.

This existing terrace was transformed into a
porch with a simple and modern steel
structure fitted with a retractable screen.

© Reto Guntli/Zapaimages

Wooden blinds can be fixed onto any
veranda structure to provide more shade or
create a more private atmosphere.

© Allain Brugier

118
Porches

© Allain Brugier

Brunete Fraccaroli created this outdoor
living area in São Paulo to make the most of
the warm Brazilian climate. Anti-reflective
glass was used for the porch ceiling to
protect the dining area without obstructing
light and views.

© Michael Saggus

© Michael Saggus

© CCS Architecture

This new, 2000-square foot house designed by CCS Architecture is set within a grove of walnut and pepper trees on a five-acre parcel in Sonoma, California. A slightly sloped roof is counterpoised with a floating metal canopy for effect and shade.

© CCS Architecture

© CCS Architecture

© JD Peterson

© CCS Architecture

125

Situated on the northeastern part of
Denmark's main island, this house opens
towards the east in the form of a traditional
porch structure to take advantage of the
natural light and ocean views.

© Hans Pattist

Situated in the Botshol of the Netherlands,
this house—designed by NIO
Architecten—presents a zinc roof
structure that juts out over an elevated
deck floor.

The raised wooden deck causes this house
to seem to float above the garden. The
slanting roof creates an unexpected porch
structure on either side of the house.

© Patrick Reynolds

Taking the form of a wooden platform, this porch is protected by the residence's roof structure, which extends out over the deck.

© Patrick Reynolds

© Jordi Miralles

© Jordi Miralles

© Jordi Miralles

Materials like concrete, glass, and wood can
generate austere structures such as this
contemporary style porch.

© Nelson Kon

An area that contains the bedrooms in this residence is raised and supported by four pillars to function as a porch structure.

© Joan Roig

An original and austere design integrates
the porch into this contemporary residence,
which is characterized by its clean lines and
defined volumes.

© Joan Roig

143

© Roger Casas

A retractable screen gives this porch versatility, allowing it to remain open to the sunlight or closed to provide shade for the outdoor living area on warmer days.

© Roger Casas

The abundant use of light colors and
materials multiplies the luminous character
of this garden and terrace.

Verandas

○ A veranda is a large balcony typically situated on the ground level. Its origin can be traced to the Hindi word barandah, a feature of the traditional architecture of Kerala consisting of an open balcony supported by pillars at the front or around a main structure. The word's relation to the Spanish word baranda, meaning "railing," suggests that the Hindi term most likely arose due to the influence of Portuguese explorers of India. Indeed, a railing is one of the main characteristics of the veranda, along with the presence of pillars or wooden posts that support a roof structure. The veranda is often synonymous with porch, although the former term is more frequently associated with the traditional antebellum of the southern United States. In some cases, a veranda is differentiated from a porch by a more enclosed nature, possibly incorporating doors, walls, or windows that allow the space to become fully interior. This attribute makes it especially apt for cooler and variable climates and areas prone to rainfall. The protection that a veranda offers from the natural elements also allows for a broader choice of materials and furnishings, which can result in an especially cozy and comfortable living space through the integration of textured fabrics, diverse light fixtures, and delicate decorative elements. Whether in the traditional style or reinterpreted within a contemporary context, the verandas shown here exemplify the potential of an exterior space to transform into unique and alternative year-round living spaces.

This partially enclosed terrace functions as an extension of the interior space and benefits from the natural light diffused by the wooden blinds.

This outdoor space in Argentina
incorporates a swinging sofa, a classic
element of typical verandas.

154

Verandas

Glass balconies provide a necessary safety
measure without hampering views of the
surrounding landscape.

© Tom Bonner

© Jordi Miralles

© Giorgio Baroni

Located on the Aeolian Islands in Italy, this veranda adopts a Moroccan style through the use of typical Moroccan rugs, cushions, and lamps.

© Miquel Tres

© Miquel Tres

The ceiling of this veranda was painted with a glossy white varnish in order to reflect the natural light and generate luminosity.

© Miquel Tres

The sheltered nature of a veranda allows for a variety of plants, from those that require more sunlight to those that only need indirect daylight.

© Miquel Tres

164

Verandas

© Jordi Sarrà

166

Verandas

© Andreas von Einsiedel

© Andreas von Einsiedel

© Andreas von Einsiedel

Limestone and wood are the main materials used to construct this veranda characterized by its luxurious atmosphere filled with comfortable sofas and armchairs.

A discreet railing allows for uninterrupted
views and a more integral relationship with
the exterior landscape.

© Ken Hayden/Redcover.com

This traditional veranda wraps around the
house to create 360 degree views of the
breathtaking mountain landscape.

© Jake Fitzjones/Redcover.com

Opting for a Moroccan style can be both
practical and stylish. Rugs, cushions, and a
few decorative details suffice.

This outdoor space fully embraces the magnificent ocean views from this coastal residence.

186

Verandas

A stone fireplace, old wooden beams, and a
mixture of decorative objects gives this
veranda a cozy and intimate feel.

The vaulted ceilings and spacious character
of this veranda allow for a variety of
sophisticated environments.

© Reto Guntli/Zapaimages

An arched doorway leads to an additional
outdoor sitting area covered with a canopy
of trees and leaves.

This veranda in Bali reflects the local
architectural style in structural details such
as the balcony railing.

© Reto Guntli/Zapaimages

© Reto Guntli/Zapaimages

Weathered furnishings and antique objects
land a rural and sophisticated air to this
outdoor space.

© Reto Guntli/Zapaimages

The tropical setting of this residence in
South America is emphasized by its use of
local materials and decorative objects.

The sheltered character of this outdoor
space, despite the absence of windows or
doors, allowed the owners to introduce all
kinds of furnishings and objects.

© Reto Guntli/Zapaimages

Existing tree trunks were used as additional support for this tall structure, giving it an organic and monumental appearance.

A simple arrangement of mattresses and
pillows can create a comfortable and
attractive exterior lounge area.

© Reto Guntli/Zapaimages

A veranda is the ideal place for a daybed in which to enjoy the warmth of the sun and the views of the outdoors.

Exquisite furnishings and rare decorative objects convert an ordinary terrace into a truly special and unique outdoor space.

Saving this large tree by building the veranda around it resulted in an original and attractive solution.

© Murray Fredericks

The open character of this lounge area is created by the dominating presence of glass and its close relationship to the exterior patio.

© Murray Fredericks

© Ron Dahlquist

The main living area of this contemporary
residence in Hawaii merges with the
exterior terrace through the use of folding
glass doors.

© Ron Dahlquist